The Jarrold Book of

The Countryside in Summer

with text by **E. A. ELLIS**

D1447684

Jarrold Colour Publications, Norwich

Summer is the season of greatest increase, when the sun's radiant energy activates plant life all through the long days and warms the air, soil and water to a degree most favourable for the well-being of animals, whether they be cattle grazing pastures, birds seeking provender for their young or insects partaking of the bounty of a world of tender leaves and honeyed blossoms. In these islands a maritime climate tends to hold sway over all, tempering the extreme heat of still, cloudless days through the generation of sea breezes before the sun has reached its zenith; but there are some inland regions where, very locally, something approaching the high day temperatures more typically associated with continental steppes are experienced from time to time, notably in East Anglia's brecklands, which have plants, insects and spiders adapted specially for survival in these conditions. Summer days lengthen to the greatest extreme in the far north, but leafing and blossoming there are not necessarily speedier on that account owing to the influence of cooling winds and, in mountainous areas, the effects of high altitude. On the whole, warmth has a swifter effect than bright illumination on plant growth and when large anticyclones bring vast pools of warm air to linger with us for long periods in the summer months it is in the south of England that vegetation responds most quickly to the kindly influence. Britain's summers are notoriously fickle, however, and although June is typically sunny, July tends on the whole to be showery and August often has intermittent spells of rain and chill winds. Differences in our summer climate year by year can have a marked effect on wildlife. When inclement weather persists over long periods coinciding with the normal times of emergence for certain butterflies, the species affected fail to propagate their kind successfully in that season and when we have a succession of poor summers it may take a long time for recovery to occur when a cycle of more favourable years comes along. In the tropics many butterflies undergo a period of dormancy in the dry season when vegetation withers in the blazing heat. In Britain some small tortoiseshell and peacock butterflies emerging at the end of July take up resting positions in hollow trees or buildings straight away and remain inactive until the following spring while others of the same species follow them into retreat in autumn. In some years many pupae from early summer caterpillars of the swallowtail produce butterflies in August, but in a dull season their emergence is mostly delayed until the following year. In exceptionally hot summers the small copper butterfly may breed continuously. Fine, warm summers produce impressive increments in the growth of timber, as can be seen when rings in cross-sections of the trunks are inspected later. Conversely little girth accrues when the season is dull and cold. Long exposure to sunshine encourages extra leaf-growth, with the result that as tree leaves fall and herbaceous vegetation dies down at the end of summer there is a corresponding wealth of tissue available for the agents of decay to deal with and eventually add to the soil's reserves of humus. In some years the weather favours the multiplication of certain insects such as aphids in early summer and there is a consequent swarming of ladybirds and hoverflies whose larvae feed on these plant lice. There are similar marked fluctuations in the numbers of many other insects, some of which, when more abundant than usual, may have severe effects on particular plants by causing defoliation or by infesting flowers and fruits. When shallow rain-pools abound there is apt to be an increase in populations of mosquitoes and biting midges; in a drought much of the countryside remains free from these blood-sucking insects. In very hot summers algal 'blooms' may develop in lakes and where waters are richly charged with nutrients from various sources of pollution the activity of microscopic organisms may create anaerobic conditions, killing fishes and other aquatic animals dependent on free oxygen for survival. In some shallow pools bacteria exploiting this situation produce toxins lethal to ducks and other water-birds, which suffer paralysis from 'botulism'. In warmed brackish waters the dinoflagellate *Prymnesium* liberates toxins which kill fishes and various invertebrate animals. Various fungal diseases of plants become prevalent in the course of the summer, depending on the impact of dry or wet weather at critical times: for instance, powdery mildews flourish in a hot season and potato blight spreads rapidly when moist westerly winds sweep over the country. When July is wet, mushrooms, giant puffballs and other fleshy fungi sprout from the soil as the moisture soaks in, but when there is a drought their appearance may be delayed until early autumn. As the corn ripens and the countryside achieves a final glory of blossoming, grasshoppers chirp in sun-scorched places, ants swarm forth on their marriage flights, the summer air is filled with minute thunder-flies (thrips) and swallows, old and young, pursue teeming insects over-head. Most birds have reared their families and many retire to moult as soon as responsibilities are at an end. Even as early as July the southward passage of bird migrants may be observed and by late August the departure of summer visitors is in full swing as may be seen most spectacularly along the coast. The bats are summer breeders, like our few reptiles. For some small mammals such as shrews the life of adults draws to a close at summer's passing. As nights lengthen and get colder, mists shroud many an August dawn, beading the thistledown, spiders' webs and grasses with moisture in sparkling beauty. Bumble-bees grow lazy at their flowery banquets; robins pierce the morning silence with brief heraldings of autumn's approach. The honeyed scent of hayfields gives place to a richer distillation of wild fruits, nuts, fungi, ferns and flowers lingering everywhere. The days of idling on sun-warmed downs and beaches are over for another year. Mists wreath the fast-chilling caps of Scotland's hills as summer flies swiftly on its way and the purple of heather across the moors, like a rainbow, spans the view between shadows of autumn's threatening clouds. Ospreys desert their eyries, lake birds move to the sea, but the golden eagles remain in their fastnesses, and thus it is with wildlife elsewhere in this varied realm which gives sanctuary to strangers in summer and winter while hardy natives hold their ground.

Hedgerows

As cow parsley runs to seed and the last petals of hawthorn fall, dog roses open in the June sunshine, grasses grow tall in shimmering beauty with the gold of buttercups in their midst and moon-daisies overtopping them. Verges become colourful with sprawling trefoils and soon there are galaxies of summer flowers appearing in swift succession to gladden the eyes of the wayfarer until August brings the final flourish of purple knapweeds and thistles, crowded with bees and butterflies. Sun-loving insects swarm everywhere, nibbling lush foliage, imbibing sap or seeking nectar and pollen. Hedgerow birds soon complete the rearing of their young and in July the cuckoo parents depart. While warblers, tits and flycatchers pursue the swarming insects, flocks of finches troop to seed-heads on wastes and verges everywhere as the season advances.

1

1. YOUNG CUCKOO (*Cuculus canorus*). Seen here in the nest of a dunnock (hedge sparrow), which is one of its commoner foster-parents, this parasitic nestling has all the attention which would have been given to the family it has supplanted. On leaving the nest, young cuckoos often cadge food from various passing birds, but eventually learn to find insects for themselves. They migrate to Africa two months later than their parents.

2. YELLOW-HAMMER (*Emberiza citrinella*). This species has a very long nesting season, breeding in hedgerows and scrub even as late as September in some years. The hair-lined grassy nest is usually built near the ground, in thick cover. The eggs are often stained pink with conspicuous purplish-black scribbly markings; they are incubated by the hen while the canary-yellow-headed cock spends much of his time uttering the characteristic 'little bit of bread and no *cheese*' song from a perch not far away. These buntings have many provincial names, some of which, like 'guler' (meaning yellow) are of ancient origin.

3. LONG-EARED BAT (*Plecotus auritus*). Readily distinguished from other British species by its very long ears, this is one of our commoner bats, present throughout the countryside, though least frequently met with in Scotland. It has a ten-inch wing span which makes it appear large in flight, although the body is relatively small. Roosting and hibernating mainly in hollow trees, but also in roofs and caves to some extent, it is adept at snatching insects such as moths flying round flowers at night and I have watched it peck sleeping house-flies from a ceiling. Single young are born in June and July at maternal roosts. Activity starts at sunset.

4. DRINKER CATERPILLAR (*Philudoria potatoria*). The name 'drinker' has come to be used for this particular caterpillar for the reason that when noticed clinging to grass early in the day, its furry coat is usually beaded with moisture from the night's dew. It would appear that the fur also provides waterproofing and this is borne out when the caterpillars are flooded on marshy ground, as they can then be seen afloat with silver bubbles of air held in the fur. The young caterpillars appear in August, but usually remain quite small until growth is resumed fully in the following spring. Many are then eaten by cuckoos. The moths emerge in April.

5. DRINKER MOTH. These emerge from tough silken cocoons attached to tall grasses and sedges in July. The males are smaller and usually more reddish brown than the females and have feathery antennae and noticeably furry legs. The sandy coloured females can sometimes be seen patrolling grassy places at dusk and dipping down here and there to extrude eggs, which are scattered over a wide area. The fast-flying males dash round at night and are often attracted by bright lights; the females are not usually dazzled in this way. Both sexes vary in colour and marking; some specimens lack cross lines or white spots on their wings.

6. PEACOCK BUTTERFLY (*Inachis io*). The black, spiky caterpillars of this species may be found in numbers living together on nettles in early summer. Butterflies from these emerge in late July and August; some go at once into shelter and remain quiescent until the following year while others visit flowers for a while and hibernate in autumn. Mating does not take place until spring.

7. COMMA (*Polygonia c-album*). Like the white admiral, this butterfly has sometimes colonised much of southern England and at other times survived only in a restricted area. The brown caterpillar has a broad white stripe on its back and feeds on nettle, currant and hop. There are two broods a year; some adults hibernate on trees and pair in spring.

6

7

10

8. LARGE WHITE (*Pieris brassicae*) CATERPILLARS. In some years these cater-pillars are plentiful on cabbages, mustard crops and the leaves of Indian cress in gardens. The eggs are laid in large batches on the plants and the larvae at first feed in close company, causing concentrated damage. In some parts of northern Europe wild colonies subsist on dittander (*Lepidium latifolium*).

9. COCOONS OF PARASITE (*Apanteles glomeratus*) FROM CATERPILLAR OF LARGE WHITE. In most years virtually all the caterpillars produced in Britain by the invading butterflies are destroyed by the larvae of *Apanteles*, a small braconid wasp. The parasites feed internally and finally eat their way out and spin clusters of silken cocoons alongside the victim's body.

10. LARGE WHITE BUTTERFLY (*Pieris brassicae*). Although often common in summer, this species depends for its presence here on the periodic arrival of migrants. sometimes in immense flocks, from overseas. Many of the invaders come from around the Baltic where wild food-plants are plentiful and the larvae are not heavily parasitised as they are in Britain. Immigration occurs chiefly in July and August.

11. CORN BINDWEED (*Convolvulus arvensis*). The white or pink fluted trumpets of this 'wheat-bine' can often be seen spread over dry ground by roadsides and in fields in great numbers during July and August, especially on grassy banks near the coast. The flowers open in sunshine and have an almond scent; at night and in dull weather they remain closed, being folded in pleats. The plants are deep-rooted and hard to eradicate.

12. JACK-GO-TO-BED-AT-NOON (*Tragopogon pratensis minus*). Also known as goatsbeard and shepherd's clock, this grassy leaved plant is widespread along roadsides, being most noticeable in early summer when the flowers open of a morning. On very sunny days they close well before noon. A tap-rooted biennial, it has edible, fleshy roots like those of purple salsify. The variety with small heads and projecting bracts is much commoner than the large one.

13. HEARTSEASE (*Viola tricolor*). The progenitor of old-fashioned garden pansies (many modern varieties are of hybrid origin) this small annual turns up here and there on open ground and in short turf, mainly where the soil is somewhat acid, in all parts of Britain. The flowers vary greatly in size and colour and have a long season. They are visited chiefly by bees and butterflies. Their provincial names include 'cats'-faces' and 'love in idleness'.

14. GIANT HOGWEED (*Heracleum mantegazzianum*). This monster umbellifer from the Caucasus is naturalised in many places. The large, jagged leaves have bristly, purple-spotted stems and a rank odour. It can be dangerous for some people with sensitive skins to handle the foliage, since the juice can produce painful blisters. Seeds germinating in spring produce young plants which are destined to flower two years later. Creamy umbels grow to a height of fifteen feet in July.

12

13

16. CORN POPPY (*Papaver rhoeas*). Masses of scarlet poppies are by no means a common sight nowadays, but here and there they may still dominate tracts of waste ground or even the occasional cornfield. The sudden reappearance in large numbers is often due to the fact that the seeds can remain alive for a great many years when buried in the soil, so that when the ground is ploughed they are able to germinate as they are brought to the surface. The flowers produce no nectar, but their numerous stamens offer quantities of pollen which is attractive to various bees and little striped wasp-like hover-flies.

17. CREEPING THISTLE (*Cirsium arvense*). A very persistent, deep-rooted perennial, this slender and rather small-flowered thistle forms extensive colonies by roadsides, in pastures, cornfields and on waste ground in open country generally throughout Britain. Large patches of it commonly develop from a single seedling, as is demonstrated clearly when one comes across the white-flowered form. The flowers are normally unisexual and although the plants may produce an abundance of fluff in late summer, few seeds develop. The flowers attract bees and butterflies and the leaves have a sweet-scented rust (*Puccinia punctiformis*).

18. DOG ROSE (*Rosa canina*). The tall, arching stems of this commonest of wild briars sprawl over hedges and appear on scrubland almost everywhere, bearing sprays of elegant blossoms in June and July. The flowers are only very faintly scented and the petals vary in tint from white to deep pink. The seeds are dispersed mainly by berry-eating birds. Many of our cultivated roses are budded or grafted on to stocks of this hardy species. Rather surprisingly dog roses seldom hybridise with garden varieties, although the famous white rose of York is said to have originated from a white, thornless *R. canina* pollinated by a damask rose.

15. COMMON MALLOW (*Malva sylvestris*). The colour 'mauve' derives its name from this flower, which grows freely by roadsides in the southern half of England, from June until autumn frosts come. The flat, rounded fruits go by the name of 'fairy cheeses' and country children often pick and eat them.

18

19. SCARLET PIMPERNEL (*Anagallis arvensis*). This common annual of open ground flowers mainly in June and July, opening only in full sunshine. Typically scarlet, with a violet circle in its 'eye', there are also white, yellowish, salmon-pink, lilac and bright blue varieties. Some plants have both red and blue flowers.

20. YARROW (*Achillea millefolium*). Common in grassy places, especially roadsides, yarrow bears white or pink flowers in late summer. Its feathery leaves are faintly aromatic. The plant has a long history as a medicinal herb, being used in tonic drinks and healing ointments. People ate its leaves in prehistoric times.

21. FLOWER CRAB-SPIDER (*Misumena vatia*). Rather like a praying mantis, this spider lies in wait to seize insects, including bees, as they alight on flowers. She spins no web, but relies on her camouflage for a chance to surprise victims. She can change colour to match white, cream, yellow·or pink flowers.

22. SEXTON BEETLES (*Necrophorus vespillo*). Several kinds of these insects are responsible for burying the dead carcases of small mammals and birds by scraping away the earth beneath. Eggs are laid and the larvae feed on the carrion, kept moist by burial. Small brown mites (*Parasitus* sp.) often cling to the beetles.

21

22

23. APHIDS ON KNAPWEED. Many kinds of sap-sucking plant lice infest vegetation all through the summer. There are winged and wingless forms in most species and in many cases there is migration from one kind of food-plant to another, during the year. Numerous generations are produced, starting with fertilised eggs in spring, after which successive batches of wingless females increase by virgin birth. Finally a winged bisexual generation appears.

24. HOVER-FLIES (*Syrphus balteatus*). Hover-flies of many sorts and sizes, mostly rather wasp-like in their markings, may be seen darting and hovering in the air and visiting flowers (mainly for pollen) on fine days in summer. Their larvae crawl about leaves, devouring aphids. *S. balteatus* is strongly migratory, sometimes appearing in great swarms along our south and east coasts in August; mass southward flights have been observed through mountain passes.

25. GREAT GREEN BUSH CRICKET (*Tettigonia viridissima*). Bush crickets can be distinguished at once from true grasshoppers and locusts by their long antennae. This is the largest species found in Britain, locally common along hedges, especially in coastal areas. The insects chirp loudly after sunset and climb bushes, also making short flights and later settling to feed mainly on leaves, but also caterpillars and snails occasionally. The females lay eggs in soil with their sword-shaped ovipositors.

26. SCORPION-FLY (*Panorpa communis*). These curiously long-beaked insects have survived as a type for many millions of years, having evolved long before moths and butterflies existed in the world. The commonest species, shown here visiting flowers, also sits about on wayside foliage in summer. The male is distinguished by its reddish, up-curled tail which somewhat resembles a scorpion's sting but is not venomous. The food includes dead insects and juices of over-ripe blackberries.

27

28

27. GOATSBEARD RUST (*Puccinia hysterium*). This fungus attacks goatsbeards commonly along roadsides, producing clustercups on leaves and stems in spring and summer, followed by skin-covered masses of dark brown teleutospores which liberate small basidiospores to infect the next crop of seedlings. .

28. GIANT PUFFBALLS (*Calvatia gigantea*). Often as large as man's head, these 'bulfers' flourish most commonly in wayside nettle beds, appearing in July and August. When young and still snow-white they are pleasantly edible, but on darkening the flavour deteriorates. The fluffy matrix of dried specimens is used as a styptic.

Waterways and Marshes

As the green of reeds begins to show in June the first yellow irises open and are followed by tassels of meadow-rue, the foam of meadowsweet and, in July and August, a host of rampant willowherbs, purple loosestrife and other tall and colourful plants. At the same time, aquatic vegetation reaches its peak of activity, supporting a wealth of microscopic creatures, while pond snails multiply and dragonflies and water-bugs abound. In June and July glow-worms light the darkness of dewy nights on fens and innumerable moths appear. Tadpoles turn into frogs and toads and leave the water along with adult newts which return to a terrestrial life after spawning. Reed-beds harbour small warblers all through the summer, while water-birds thrive on an abundance of food and shoals of fish-fry grow quickly in our lakes and rivers.

29. REED WARBLER (*Acrocephalus scirpaceus*). This summer visitor comes every year in large numbers to areas where there are extensive reed beds fringing lakes and rivers and it is notably common round the Norfolk Broads. Its nest is a neat grassy cup woven round reed stalks, often lined with sallow fluff and usually over water. It can be distinguished easily by its plain olive-brown plumage from the dark-streaked sedge-warbler and its churring song is less strident.

30

30. SEDGE WARBLER (*Acrocephalus schoenobaenus*). Often adopting much drier and more bushy habitats than the reed warbler, this species comes to marshy places all over Britain to nest in summer. It is more addicted than the other to rising a few feet in butterfly-like flights which are a feature of nuptial display.

31. HARVEST MICE (*Micromys minutus*). Although traditionally associated with cornfields, this little red mouse has its normal home in reedy and sedgy habitats. Once regarded as confined largely to the south and east of England, recent research has shown it to be much more common and widespread.

32. ELEPHANT HAWK MOTH (*Deilephila elpenor*). This insect gets its name from the weird caterpillar which has large eye-like markings behind the head and a 'trunk'. The larva is common on willowherbs and bedstraws in marshes and the moth flies in June and July, being attracted by honeysuckle and other tubular flowers.

33. REED DAGGER CATERPILLAR (*Semyra albovenosa*). These feed on various tall marsh grasses and sometimes on the flowering plumes of reeds, chiefly in the fens and broads of East Anglia. Two broods of the moths emerge in June and August. The fore wings are pale cream and veined and the hind ones white.

32

33

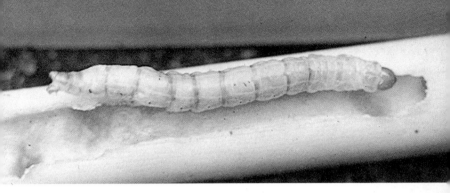

36

34. BULRUSH WAINSCOT CATERPILLAR (*Nonagria typhae*). The greater reed-mace is commonly attacked by this species in most parts of England, though less frequently in the north. The moth makes small slits in the soft stalks for the insertion of her eggs. The smooth, translucent, yellowish or pink larvae devour the pith in the stems and eventually pupate within the hollows they have excavated. Plants attacked turn yellow and die back, failing to produce flowering 'pokers'.

35. BULRUSH WAINSCOT. This moth emerges from chrysalids in reed-mace stalks mainly in August and September (see Plate 34 for an account of the caterpillar). It is widely distributed in Britain and often locally abundant except in some northern areas. Commonly a rather dingy brown in general coloration, it is sometimes reddish or almost black. The chrysalids of this species, though neatly hidden in silk-plugged chambers, are often destroyed by birds.

36. FLAME WAINSCOT (*Senta flammea*). The narrow, sharply angled fore wings of this small wainscot moth distinguish it from numerous other species with similar protective coloration resembling the pale straw tints of dead reeds. The earliest of its tribe to appear, it is found from May to July in local abundance in the vast reedy fens of Cambridge, Huntingdon and east Norfolk. The caterpillars feed on reed leaves at night and hide in the stems by day.

37

38

39

37. PURPLE LOOSESTRIFE (*Lythrum salicaria*). This tall and showy plant abounds alongside our lowland rivers and canals where it is conspicuous in July and August. The flowers are of three distinct forms, designed to facilitate cross-pollination.

38. HEMP AGRIMONY (*Eupatorium cannabinum*). Large patches of this tall marsh perennial with hemp-like leaves bear dusky pink blossoms in late summer. Like the purple buddleias of our gardens, they are very attractive to butterflies.

39. YELLOW WATER-LILY (*Nuphar lutea*). Our commonest water-lily, this species develops massive and persistent rootstock. The plump, poppy-like fruits emerge from the water and eventually decay, releasing jelly-bags of black seeds.

40. COMMON MARSH ORCHID (*Dactylorhiza praetermissa*). Plentiful in many water-meadows and fenny places in the southern half of England, this species has unspotted leaves. The flowers are usually purplish, but may be pale pink or white.

41

41. WHITE WATER-LILY (*Nymphaea alba*). This 'water rose', as it was known in medieval times, abounds in fairly deep pools and lakes which it prefers to running waters. The giant leaves or 'pads' are green and glossy above and purple underneath and may have stalks up to ten feet long. At the height of summer some of the leaves may be furled to one side by puffs of wind. The 'brandy-bottle' fruits bob at the surface of the water for a while but later becomes submerged and liberate pink seeds.

42. GREATER REED-MACE (*Typha latifolia*). The massive reddish-brown or almost black 'pokers' of this widespread swamp plant develop in late summer and remain standing all through the winter after the leaves have died. The winds of March then usually cause them to burst into billows of white, fluffy seeds. These are apt to be carried long distances by air and in this way the plant has achieved an almost world-wide distribution, being a rapid colonist of mud wherever this is exposed round the edges of lakes and ponds.

43

44

43. WATER BISTORT (*Polygonum amphibium*). This amphibious plant grows very adaptably in waters of varying depth, so that it can survive when ponds and lakes dry out from time to time. In deep water, long-stalked floating leaves develop. The bright pink flower heads appear above water in July and August.

44. WATER MINT (*Mentha aquatica*). The peppermint often noticeable as one treads marshy ground comes from the leaves of this very common plant. The flowers come very late in summer and attract many honey-bees and butterflies. The garden peppermint is a hybrid between this species and the common green spearmint.

45. GLOW-WORMS (*Lampyris noctiluca*). Maturing in early June, these insects are active on dewy summer nights. The males are fully winged beetles and are attracted by the brilliantly luminous wingless females which climb the grass and twirl their tail-lamps invitingly. Nowadays many of the males fly to artificial lights and the population has suffered accordingly. The luminosity is produced by luciferin as in most other phosphorescent organisms. Glow-worm larvae look much like the adult females and display spots of light. They feed on snails, first inflicting a poisonous bite and then liquidising the victims chemically.

46. MUSK BEETLE (*Aromia moschata*). As their name implies, these large long-horn beetles emit a powerful musky scent which reveals their presence among riverside willows where they breed. Even the larvae, feeding in dead boughs and trunks, disseminate this odour, like those of the wood-boring caterpillars of goat-moths. The beetles squeak rather like an old pair of bellows, the sound being made by the edges of head and thorax rubbing together. They behave in this way when alarmed by handling. An inch and a quarter in length, they vary from metallic bronze to green and peacock-blue in colour. Marsh flowers are visited in summer.

47. HORSE-FLY (*Tabanus distinguendus*). These blood-sucking insects are often too numerous for human comfort in marshy places in the heat of summer. Only the females bite and draw blood from various animals while the males visit flowers for nectar. They are powerful fliers and the wings produce a rather low droning sound as they approach a victim. In life, their eyes are brilliantly iridescent. Besides several large *Tabanus* species there are the smaller, greyish, 'clegs' (*Haematopota*) and yellow and black 'harlequin-flies' (*Chrysops*). The carnivorous larvae live mostly in marshy ground.

48. SCARCE DARTER DRAGONFLY (*Libellula fulva*). Flying over still pools and ditches in June and July, this species has a patchy distribution in the south and east of England, in the Fens, the Norfolk Broads and the boggy pools of Dorset. The tawny female is shown here, with dark basal wing markings and black abdominal stripe. The male acquires a pale powder-blue bloom on its abdomen and is a more slender insect. Young males are tawny.

49. SMOOTH NEWT (*Triturus vulgaris*). This is our commonest and most widely distributed newt or 'eft' and one of the few amphibians also found in Ireland. After breeding in ponds in spring the adults leave the water. By day they can only be found by searching under logs and stones or at the moist bases of grass and moss tufts. By night they crawl forth to feed on worms, slugs and insects. Very occasionally tadpoles trapped in waters deep underground remain aquatic and retain their gills as adults, some being very light-coloured or even white.

50. AMBER SNAIL (*Succinea putris*). This is the commonest of the translucent, amber-shelled amphibious snails found climbing reeds and other waterside vegetation. They are eaten by water shrews and various birds, including water-rails, moorhens, ducks, pheasants and wood pigeons. They are often parasitised by flies and at times the green- or orange-banded larvae of a kind of fluke-worm can be seen wriggling in a distended tentacle. This parasite (*Distomum macrostomum*) undergoes further development when swallowed, as intended, by a marsh bird.

51. EGG-COCOON OF SPIDER

(*Tetragnatha extensa*). In summer it is common to find flattish silken discs attached to the upper surfaces of reed and sedge leaves overhanging the water of rivers, pools and ditches. These may be almost white at first, but soon turn greenish grey or black as the eggs mature. Eventually, after the young spiders have escaped, they have a honey-combed appearance. The adult spiders have long, slender, tapering bodies tinted various shades of green, brown, rust, yellow, black and silver and they are neatly camouflaged as they sit with long legs stretched in front and behind along the length of a narrow leaf.

52. SPIDER FUNGUS (*Gibellula aranearum*).

If a search is made in the grassy undergrowth of marshes during the summer months, many spiders will be found dead, clinging to the undersides of leaves, with this fungus sprouting from their bodies. Both young and adult spiders are parasitised and even the egg clusters may be attacked. The victims become infected through contact with the very small dusty spores. These develop a network of mycelial strands and, when the spider dies, produce a white or canary-yellow layer from which long, slender 'fingers' emerge, set with whorls of clustered spores.

52

53. ORCHID MOULD (*Cladosporium orchidis*).

This parasitic fungus forms extensive and often circular dark brown or black blotches on living leaves of the common marsh orchid (*Dactylorhiza praetermissa*) in summer. Although locally frequent in some of the marshes surrounding the Norfolk Broads, where it was first discovered in 1945, it seems to have escaped notice elsewhere and has not been reported attacking any other type of orchid. The thin, dark-veined mycelial mats give rise to erect sporophores crowned with small branches budding off short chains of spores. The non-parasitic sooty brown mould *Cladosporium herbarum* is widespread.

55

54. REED CIGAR GALL OF *LIPARA LUCENS*. Sluggish, rather hump-backed flies lay eggs in young reed shoots in spring and their grubs feed in the stalks, forming closely placed leafy galls in summer. Often smaller 'guest' flies share the accommodation and various parasitic hymenoptera attack the inmates. Twenty-five different kinds of insects have been found associated with these galls, mostly emerging from them in spring. Old, empty galls are sometimes used as nest-chambers by small bees.

55. MEADOWSWEET RUST (*Triphragmium ulmariae*). The bright orange, powdery aecidiospores of this fungus appear in conspicuous masses distorting the stems and veins of meadowsweet leaves in early summer. Smaller, pale yellow clusters of uredospores develop on the undersides of the leaves later, followed by dark brown (appearing black) three-celled, warty, triangular teleutospores which persist through the winter. This rust is common in Britain.

56. STRIPE SMUT (*Ustilago longissima*). A common parasite of broad-leaved sweet-grass (*Glyceria maxima*) and flote-grass (*G. fluitans*). Long, parallel lines of yellowish-brown powdery spherical spores erupt in summer and may be dispersed by wind, rain, insects and browsing snails.

57. CUTTING RIVER WEEDS. Although rooted aquatic plants contribute much to the health of rivers and are essential for the well-being of fishes and other creatures, their growth under the influence of summer sunshine may impede the flow and obstruct navigation; so, periodic cutting is undertaken by responsible authorities.

Coast

Cushions of thrift and sea campion adorn our sea cliffs in June and later, dunes and shingle banks become gay with a succession of flowers peculiar to coastal habitats. Most salt-marsh plants bloom in July and August, some of them providing fine displays of colour, notably the sea lavenders and, later, the sea aster. Many butterflies flourish on dunes and in August, especially, the blue flowers of sea-holly are a great attraction for them. On our south and east coasts numbers of migrant insects commonly arrive from overseas at this season: not only various butterflies, but also humming-bird hawk moths, hover-flies and dragonflies. Many seabirds are still busy nesting and rearing chicks in early summer and common seals have their pups at this time. Grasshoppers on coastal dunes reach a peak of activity in August.

58. COMMON TERN (*Sterna hirundo*). Several thousands of these 'sea-swallows' nest on Britain's beaches, most abundantly on East Anglian nature reserves. In early summer there is great activity in the colonies as the parents keep flying in with whitebait and small sand-eels for their growing chicks. Clouds of screaming birds flutter overhead, diving fiercely at intruders. At the end of the season these terns migrate southwards, following the Atlantic coast to Equatorial waters.

59. COMMON SEAL (*Phoca vitulina*). These delightful and highly intelligent mammals breed chiefly on sandbanks and quiet beaches, the females giving birth to single pups usually in June. The young are able to take to the water immediately, but need to be suckled for some time afterwards and those which become separated from their mothers are apt to come ashore in a starving condition. Although often persecuted by fishermen, their feeding habits do not warrant this except possibly where they are very numerous on restricted fishing grounds.

60. PAINTED LADY (*Cynthia cardui*). Varying numbers of these far-ranging migrant butterflies reach us from the Mediterranean region in summer, producing spiky caterpillars on thistles. Some of their offspring undertake a return migration.

61. FIVE-SPOT BURNET MOTH (*Zygaena trifolii*). Various gay little burnet moths, flying heavily like bumble-bees, may be seen visiting flowers on dunes, downs and fens on sunny days in summer.

62. GROUND LACKEY CATERPILLARS (*Malacosoma castrensis*). These softly furry caterpillars feed colonially in webs on tidal salt-marshes of south-east England from May to July. The plump-bodied sandy to reddish-brown moths appear in July.

63. SEA PEA (*Lathyrus japonicus maritimus*). Rooting deeply in shingle, chiefly along the south coast and in East Anglia, this perennial plant shows blue-green foliage almost throughout the year and blooms from June to August.

64. SEA BINDWEED (*Calystegia soldanella*). This is a sprawling, long-rooted perennial of coastal sands. Its fluted pink and white trumpets are conspicuous from June to September and are visited by hawk moths, bumble-bees and bee-flies.

65. SEA CAMPION (*Silene maritima*). The massed white flowers of this seaside bladder-campion are conspicuous on beach shingle and cliff ledges at midsummer. The woody rootstocks are long lived.

66. TAMARISK (*Tamarix gallica*). The tamarisks are feathery, tough shrubs with small, scale-like leaves and spikes of numerous small white or pink flowers. In this country they are often to be found well established in sandy places near the sea, especially along our south and east coasts, where they have in the first place been planted to provide wind-breaks. They are well fitted to withstand exposure to strong winds and salt spray. On hot days the leaves sparkle with minute crystals of salt exuded by their pores; at night these crystals attract moisture from the air and deliquesce; some of the moisture is absorbed by the leaves. *T. gallica*, a native of the western Mediterranean, tends to have bright green foliage and the petals, not more than two millimetres long, soon drop. The more blue-green *T. africana*, also present on our south coast, has slightly larger petals which do not fall so readily. Seeds are seldom produced here.

67. YELLOW HORNED-POPPY (*Glaucium flavum*). This is a tall and very attractive member of our seashore flora, growing chiefly in shingle. It has a wide but patchy distribution, being most plentiful along parts of our south and east coasts. Usually behaving as a biennial, although sometimes persisting longer, it has rosettes of large crinkled leaves which have a frosted appearance due to the presence of silvery hairs. These may be seen in winter. In summer stems up to a yard high bear a succession of large butter-yellow blossoms from June to September; the individual flowers last only one day and although they possess no nectar, bees and hover-flies come to them for pollen. They are succeeded by very long, horn-like green pods (sometimes attacked by linnets for the seeds even before they are ripe). All parts of the plant contain an acrid and rank-smelling orange-yellow latex which is noxious to grazing mammals. Like the similar juice of greater celandine, this has a reputation for soothing bruises and has narcotic properties.

68

69

68. COMMON SEA LAVENDER
(*Limonium vulgare*). The violet-blue
flowers of this plant appear in vast
numbers covering salt-marshes, especially along our east coast, in July and
August. Even when almost submerged
at high tide, bees can be seen flying
across the water to visit them. The
pointed, tongue-shaped leaves grow in
rosettes from blackish, fleshy rootstocks.

69. MARSH MALLOW (*Althaea offi-
cinalis*). A velvety perennial with pale
grey-green leaves and delicate pinkish
flowers, this plant grows in large clumps
along the banks of estuaries mainly in
the south and east of England. It
thrives best on clay near slightly brackish
water and flowers in August. The white,
mucilaginous roots have been used to
make 'marsh mallow' toffee.

70. TOWNSEND'S CORD-GRASS
(*Spartina townsendii*). This grass originated as a fertile hybrid between an
American and a British species on the
south coast of England about a hundred
years ago. It has invaded soft mud-flats
in our estuaries on a major scale in
recent years and helped to reclaim much
tidal land. Unfortunately it is difficult
to control.

**71. GALLS OF *Aylax hieracii* ON
UMBELLATE HAWKWEED.** Exten-
sive patches of this tall perennial hawkweed grow in sandy places inland and on
dunes. In summer it is common to find
the stems swollen into pithy lumps con-
taining numerous white larvae of a gall-
wasp. The galls turn brown and the adult
insects eat their way out in time to lay
eggs in the new shoots in spring.

72. COAST LEAF-CUTTER (*Mega-
chile maritima*). Seen here visiting flowers
of carline thistle, this 'solitary' bee lives
mainly near the sea. In summer the
female makes burrows in sandy soil and
cuts segments from leaves, using them
to fashion green cigar-like cell-packs.
Each section contains an egg and a store
of nectar and pollen as food for the larva.
Other leaf-cutters cut rounded pieces
from rose leaves in gardens.

73. PISAN SNAIL (*Theba pisana*) ON RAGWORT. Named from Pisa (of the leaning tower) where it was first described, this snail is able to flourish in dry, sandy places, including arid country round the Mediterranean and in north-west Africa. It also occurs along the Atlantic coast of France as far north as the Channel Islands and is plentiful on dunes, cliffs and waste ground near the sea in a few places in south-west Britain and the east of Ireland. In summer, during hot, sunny weather, swarms of these snails can be seen clinging to ragwort, thistles, sea kale, sea holly and other coast plants, the animals being sealed within their shells to avoid desiccation.

74. PISAN SNAILS ACTIVE. These dune snails have thick shells about eighteen millimetres wide, with dark spiral bands and are usually pink inside the mouth. Colonies of milk-white specimens occur in some places. In rainy weather, both by day and night, they feed on dead and living plants and are also recorded as predators on other snails. In dry spells they become immobile, either clustering on vegetation or, especially when the sand is blowing in windy weather, burying themselves in sand and litter. They have become pests where they have been introduced in certain parts of North America and South Africa. They are also known as white or sandhill snails.

Woodlands

Broad-leaved trees become thickly clothed with foliage in June and make great demands on soil moisture; at the same time they throw the under-growth into shade, so that few flowers can develop beneath them during the summer, although there are some exceptions, notably several of the orchids of limestone woods, while in damp situations ferns flourish in the shade. A few trees bloom in summer, including the limes and sweet chestnut. Immense numbers of moth caterpillars feed on tree foliage everywhere and several fine woodland butterflies are active at the height of summer. After the end of July most woodland birds fall rather silent, but the crooning of doves and pigeons continues. The insects abounding on trees at this season make provision for a great many fledgling birds. Many timber beetles and sawflies appear in June and July.

75. WOOD PIGEON (*Columba palumbus*). Also known as the 'ring dove', this species is met with in every part of the British Isles throughout the year. Although nesting can occur in every month, the main breeding season is in July and August, when most grain is available. The nests, built flimsily of twigs, are usually placed fairly high in trees. Only two white eggs are laid. Cooing and wing-clapping in flight are much indulged in at nesting time.

76. TURTLE DOVE (*Streptopelia turtur*). Turtle-doves are abundant summer visitors to copses and scrub-lands in England and Wales, arriving at the end of April and departing in September. In flight, the white band tipping the tail is conspicuous and they differ from the collared doves recently established here in having bright orange-brown, dark-streaked plumage over the wings and neatly rounded black and white barred patches on either side of the neck. Their rhythmic purring notes are also distinctive and may be heard all through the summer. Small twiggy nests are hidden in bushes and normally two pairs of young are reared each season.

77. JAYS (*Garrulus glandarius*). These gaily coloured birds of the crow family are typically inhabitants of oak forests, but now occupy a variety of woodlands, large and small. They have managed to survive despite centuries of attempted control by gamekeepers. In the breeding season they take eggs and young of other birds, but also feed on insects, berries and seeds. In autumn they make full use of acorns, often hiding them in grassland where some remain to grow into trees. Normally broods of five young are reared in twiggy platform-nests in bushes and trees chosen for their close cover.

78. SPOTTED FLYCATCHER (*Muscicapa striata*). This small brown bird with a streaked breast, sharp, bristle-fringed beak and large, bright, watchful eyes, is a regular summer visitor to many gardens and woodland glades. Arriving later than most other immigrants, it soon sets about building or repairing a nest in a wall cranny or tree-trunk niche and usually rears two broods in rapid succession during June and July. Perching where it commands a view of open ground, it makes numerous sallies in pursuit of insects ranging from small midges to large butterflies and dragonflies. It departs for north-east Africa about the end of August.

78

79

80

79. WHITE ADMIRAL (*Ladoga camilla*). Strictly an inhabitant of deciduous woodlands, this butterfly is on the wing from late June to early August. It may be seen visiting bramble flowers in glades or fluttering about tree-tops in the sunshine. At various periods it has increased and reduced its range in southern England. The young caterpillars hibernate between leaves.

80. PURPLE EMPEROR (*Apatura iris*). This large resplendent butterfly inhabits several of England's old oak forests where sallows are available as food for the caterpillars. Appearing from mid-July, through August, the iridescent males patrol the tops of favourite tall 'king' trees. The less colourful females tend to linger about sallow bushes where they will lay eggs.

81. BUFF-TIP (*Phalera bucephala*). This common woodland moth flies by night in June and July. When resting by day it relies on its remarkable camouflage to escape detection by foraging birds. With the wings folded it resembles a broken twig with pale buff rounded tips at both ends. The downy yellow and black striped caterpillars feed in companies on the foliage of various trees.

82. LILAC BEAUTY (*Apeira syringaria*). The caterpillars of this species may be found on privet and honeysuckle in spring in many parts of England, Wales and Ireland. They have two large horns on the back and are variegated with yellow, red and violet. The moths fly in July and resemble faded leaves, not only in colouring, but in their vein-like stripes.

82

83. PINE SAWFLY (*Diprion pini*). Swarms of these larvae commonly defoliate shoots of Scots pine in summer. On reaching full growth they drop to the ground and spin cocoons among the fallen needles. The adult insects have broad bodies, the males being black, with feathery antennae while females are twice as large, marked yellow and black, with thread-like antennae.

83

84

84. LEAST BURDOCK (*Arctium minus*). Often plentiful round margins of woods and in open glades, this species blooms in August. The small narrow-waisted heads and slender, black-mottled seeds are distinctive. The prickly heads catch on fur and clothing. The seeds are often taken by goldfinches, bullfinches and marsh tits.

85. FOXGLOVE (*Digitalis purpurea*). Both purple and white foxgloves grace open woodlands throughout Britain, favouring acid soils. The spots inside the flowers guide bumble-bees to nectar at the bottom. A 'monstrous' form has a large open bell at the top. The plants contain digitalin, valuable medicinally as a heart stimulant.

86. HONEYSUCKLE (*Lonicera periclymenum*). The fragrant woodbine entwines trees and bushes and from June to August its flowers scent the air deliciously, especially at night, when they attract long-tongued moths. By day, small hover-flies may be seen removing pollen from the projecting stamens.

87. RED CAMPION (*Silene dioica*). The magenta flowers of 'soldiers' buttons' brighten woodland glades in June. Sometimes they hybridise with white campions growing on near-by arable land and give rise to pale pink intermediates. The decorative brown seed-capsules survive on dead stems all winter.

86

7

88. WOOD PIMPERNEL (*Lysimachia nemorum*). This species spreads over the ground in damp woods and blooms continuously from May to September, especially in grassy glades where sunlight can reach it.

89. BORRER'S FERN (*Dryopteris pseudomas*). Although much resembling the common male fern, this differs in the stems being clothed with golden-brown scales, while the yellow-green segments have 'square' tips.

90. TREE SLUG (*Lehmannia marginata*). One often sees silvery slime left by these molluscs on tree-trunks which they ascend at night to feed on green algal dust, lichens and fungi. In moist weather they move with considerable speed. Some have lairs under loose bark, but usually they retire to mossy hide-outs below.

91. PARENT-BUGS (*Elasmuch grisea*). This fairly common sap-sucking shield-bug lives on the foliage of birch trees. After hibernation and mating, the females each lay a batch of eggs on the underside of a leaf, thereafter tending them and the young insects until they have completed their development.

92. SPOTTED LONGHORN (*Strangalia armata*). Various long-horn beetles (Cerambycidae) have larvae which bore tunnels in either living or dead tree-trunks. Those of this common species do not damage forest timber but feed in very rotten boughs and stumps, especially birch, willow and alder. The beetles may be seen visiting the flowers of hogweed and other umbellifers in June and July.

93. DOWN-LOOKER FLY (*Rhagio scolopacea*). These fairly large, long-legged, spotted-winged flies are peculiar in their habit of settling head-downwards on tree-trunks, usually a few feet off the ground. The reason for this behaviour is not known. They are common in lightly wooded country. The long cylindrical larvae burrow in rotten wood and leaf-litter and are said to feed on worms.

94. DRYAD'S SADDLE (*Polyporus squamosus*). Also known as the scaly polypore, this firm, leathery fungus develops asymmetrically on tree-stumps and dying trunks at various heights during the summer, often producing tiers of brackets up to fifteen inches broad. The dark feathery scales are distinctive. This species grows commonly on elm, ash and sycamore.

95. ELM-WOOD MUSHROOM (*Agaricus vinosobrunneus*). The term 'mushroom' is applied to pleasantly edible fungi of the genus *Agaricus*, characterised by the free gills, dark chocolate spore-prints, firm flesh and ringed stalk. There are about forty British species. The one illustrated grows under elms and tends to become purplish red on the streaky scaled cap.

96. OAK ROOT GALLS (unisexual *Biorhiza pallida*). The winged gall-wasps emerging from withered oak-apples in summer insert eggs in oak roots just under the surface of the ground. The resulting larvae form scaly root galls which persist for two years, eventually producing wingless parthenogenetic females whose offspring in turn are responsible for oak-apples.

97. ACORN GALLS (*Cynips quercuscalicis*). Although long known in much of southern Europe and the Channel Islands, these crinkly, crested galls of acorn cups have become widely familiar in England only very recently. Their rapid spread may have been favoured by a succession of mild winters. It has been suggested that an alternating generation occurs on Turkey oaks, but the species persists efficiently on English oaks.

98. FLOWERS OF TAN (*Fuligo septica*). This bright canary-yellow or occasionally red slime-mould develops large and conspicuous crusts on very rotten tree-trunks mainly when showery weather is followed by a fine warm spell in summer. It received its common name when it used to appear freely on the heaps of oak bark used in tanning-pits. The ripe spores are black and dusty.

**99**

10

99. TAR-SPOT OF SYCAMORE. The round black patches conspicuous on leaves of sycamore and occasionally field maple in summer are produced by a cup-fungus (*Rhytisma acerinum*). At first only conidia are produced; the grey-crusted apothecial fungus matures after the leaves have fallen and lain on the ground through the winter.

100. RESIN-TOP RUST (*Peridermium pini*). This parasite grows perennially on Scots pine, forming cankers and producing quantities of conspicuous orange clustercups on the boughs in summer. Notably a troublesome disease in Scotland (especially the Spey Valley) it has spread to conifer plantations in England.

Moors and Heaths

Moors and heaths become most richly colourful as summer advances. First we see the green of young bracken, snowy sheets of bog-cotton and the rosy tint of bilberry bells and later, the glory of heathers and bog asphodel, while the mosses have their sundews and special orchids. On hot summer days we look for a variety of brown butterflies whose larvae are reared on heath grasses. Lizards and adders bask in the sunshine and tiger-beetles scuttle over bare sandy places. Curlew, golden plover still haunt the great open wastes with their young for a while and summer visitors such as wheatear, whinchat and ring-ouzel remain until the end of the season. Wide-ranging birds of prey such as buzzards and harriers patrol the moors throughout the summer, while the ospreys of Scotland's lochs also linger until late August.

101. RABBIT (*Oryctogalus cuniculus*). Evidence strongly suggests that these animals became established in Britain only after their introduction by the Normans. At first they were bred for food and fur on private warrens known as coney garths and eventually colonised sandy heaths and woodlands everywhere. The young, known as 'kittens', are born blind and tended by the mothers at night in separate burrows. Since 1953 the population has fluctuated through myxomatosis.

10

104

102. RED-BACKED SHRIKE (*Lanius cristatus*). This rufous-brown 'butcher-bird' is a decreasing summer visitor met with nowadays mainly on brambly heaths in the south and east of England. It preys on bees, wasps, beetles, dragonflies and the occasional lizard and often hangs superfluous victims in a 'larder' on a thorn bush or barbed wire. It migrates to north-east Africa for the winter.

103. SILVER-STUDDED BLUE (*Plebejus argus*). Flying in July and August, this species can be found in local abundance on gorsy heaths in several parts of England, but is by no means a common insect nowadays. There is only one brood in the year. The eggs laid in summer do not hatch until the following spring, when the caterpillars feed mainly on gorse and heather.

104. SCOTCH ARGUS (*Erebia aethiops*). This single-brooded butterfly abounds on rough, grassy hillsides over much of Scotland and some of the northern English counties. It is on the wing throughout August, but only flies in sunshine. Eggs are laid on purple moor-grass (*Molinia caerulea*). They hatch in autumn and the young caterpillars hibernate, continuing growth in the following spring.

105. CINNABAR MOTH (*Tyria jacobaeae*). This day-flying species is most abundant on grass-heaths and wherever common ragwort flourishes. It appears mainly in June and although a weak flier, commonly makes use of the wind for its dispersal over the country-side. As a 'drift-migrant' it has been found up to thirty miles out at sea on occasion.

106. CINNABAR CATERPILLARS. These conspicuous larvae can often be found swarming on the common rag-wort (*Senecio jacobaea*) in July and August, and since this plant is poisonous to livestock, its wholesale destruction by these insects is welcomed. The cater-pillars have also been found feeding on Oxford ragwort (*S. squalidus*) and com-mon groundsel (*S. vulgaris*).

107. PUPAE OF CINNABAR MOTH. When full-fed, the caterpillars go to ground and pupate either in the loose plant litter or just under the soil surface. The chrysalids are at first bright yellow, then orange, red and finally dark brown. Like the vividly coloured moths and larvae, they are said to be rejected after sampling by insectivorous birds owing to their secretion of nauseous fluids.

108. BLOOD-DROP EMLETS (*Mimulus luteus*). Many a burn and boggy pool in Scotland and northern England is fringed with these resplen-dent trumpet-flowers in late summer. Introduced from Chile early in the nineteenth century, this plant has be-come widely naturalised like its sparsely spotted relative, the monkey-flower from North America.

109. TORMENTIL (*Potentilla erecta*). Distinguished from our other small-flowered species of *Potentilla* by its trefoil leaves, this is a common perennial plant of peatlands throughout Britain. The wiry, reddish rootstocks are crowned by dense rosettes of foliage which die down as flowering shoots develop. The blossoms make a brilliant show in sunny situations from June to September.

106

110. HEATH SPOTTED ORCHID

(*Dactylorhiza ericetorum*). One of a group of orchids with spreading, finger-like tubers, this species occurs widely on wet, acid heaths and moors, being most numerous in the north and west of Britain. The leaves are usually narrower and more lightly spotted than those of the spotted orchid common on less acid soils. The flowers are mostly pale lilac with broad, freckled lips, appearing between May and August.

111. LING (*Calluna vulgaris*).

Our commonest heather, flourishing on acid peat and sand in both lowland and upland districts. It forms large bushy hummocks which have an active life of about twenty-five years. Periodic burning stimulates new growth to provide good grazing for sheep and grouse. Besoms used to be made from the springy twigs. The crowded pearly flowers contain much nectar and attract many kinds of bees and flies.

112. DORSET HEATH (*Erica ciliaris*).

This graceful heather inhabits the extreme west of Europe bordering the Atlantic. In Britain it is confined to a few damp, sandy heaths in Dorset, Devon and Cornwall. The stems are downy and the leaves, fringed with fine hairs, are usually in whorls of three. The flowers appear from June to September and have dark, narrow mouths with pin-like styles protruding. In Dorset this species sometimes hybridises with the cross-leaved heath.

113. BOG ASPHODEL (*Narthecium ossifragum*).

The great mossy bogs of Scotland, Ireland, Wales and western England are starry with the gleaming flowers of this plant from July to September. As autumn approaches, orange-coloured capsules ripen and the stems turn red. It used to be said that this plant was the cause of sheep-rot (*ossifragum* means 'bone-breaker'), but this has been proved untrue. The seeds have forked beaks which help them to float in times of flood.

114. ROSE BAY *(Epilobium angustifolium)*. The magenta spires of this tall willow-herb make a brilliant show on the drier parts of many heaths and wastes in July and August. It was relatively rare in Britain until the present century and owes its increase to its habit of readily colonising burnt ground.

115. ROSE-BAY SEEDING. The silk-plumed seeds of this 'fireweed' drift over the countryside in late summer and autumn and establish new colonies especially where careless visitors have set fire to heaths and forests during the summer. This plant flourished on waste ground in fire-ravaged towns during World War 2.

116. BOG PIMPERNEL *(Anagallis tenella)*. This lowly creeping plant is often plentiful in mossy turf round bog pools and where landsprings produce 'flushes' in peaty valleys. It requires open, sunny habitats which are at the same time perpetually moist, and is quick to vanish when fens and bogs are drained. The delicate pink blossoms form glistening carpets in summer. Although the plants may fail to appear in a dry season, long-lasting seeds ensure recovery later.

116

117

117. HEATH-BRAT *(Dilta littoralis)*. The most primitive insects known are Thysanura or 'bristle-tails', typified by the domestic 'silver-fish' which scuttles over floors at night. Similar forms existed 360,000,000 years ago. Coppery fire-brats frequent stoves, rock-brats inhabit sea coasts and heath-brats nibble heather.

118. TOAD FLY (*Lucilia bufonivora*). Like the closely related bluebottles, most species of *Lucilia* (greenbottles) breed in the flesh of dead animals and may be regarded as useful scavengers except for their activities in relation to meat and fish intended for human consumption. However, some give trouble to sheep from time to time when the larvae infest wounds. The species illustrated has adopted a predatory habit, specialising in attacks on toads and occasionally frogs. The female lays a cluster of eggs on the hind part of the intended victim's body, keeping out of range of the creature's tongue which might otherwise snap her up. When the eggs hatch, the maggots, which may number up to a hundred, make their way swiftly to the toad's head, wriggling into the eye-sockets and entering the tissues at the back of the nose. They then develop at the toad's expense and eventually devour their host.

119. HEATH ORB-SPIDER (*Araneus quadratus*). This large spider is distinguished by the four white spots forming the points of a square on the upper surface of its abdomen. The female may grow to a length of over fifteen millimetres and is commonly of a bright orange-red colour, although yellowish or rich, dark brown on occasion. Like the common cross or 'diadem' spider of gardens, she constructs a beautiful 'geometric' web on a radial pattern, with gum-beaded spirals designed to trap flies. From the loosely meshed centre of the web there stretches a strand rather like an angler's line, reaching to the spider's separate lair in a silken tent woven near by in the gorse, heather or bramble bush chosen as a vantage point. There the spider lurks, ready to dart forth whenever a struggling insect vibrates the web. She seizes the victim, injecting poison with her fangs until its struggles cease, then wraps it in a shroud of silk, takes it to her retreat and sucks it dry.